Under the Lemon Tree

Previous Works by George Scarbrough

POETRY

Tellico Blue (first edition, E. P. DUTTON, 1949)
Tellico Blue (second edition, IRIS PRESS, 1999)
The Course is Upward (E. P. DUTTON, 1951)
Summer, So-Called (E. P. DUTTON, 1956)
New and Selected Poems (IRIS PRESS, 1977)
Invitation to Kim (IRIS PRESS, 1989)

Novels

A Summer Ago (first edition, ST. LUKE'S PRESS, 1986)
A Summer Ago (second edition, IRIS PRESS, 2011)

Under the Lemon Tree

Poems

George Scarbrough

Edited by Robert B. Cumming and Rebecca P. Mobbs

Iris Press
Oak Ridge, Tennessee

Iris Press
an imprint of the Iris Publishing Group, Inc

www.irisbooks.com

Design: Robert B Cumming, Jr.

Library of Congress Cataloging-in-Publication Data

Scarbrough, George, 1915-
 Under the lemon tree : poems / George Scarbrough ; edited by Robert B.
Cumming and Rebecca Passmore Mobbs.
    p. cm.
 ISBN 978-1-60454-214-1 (pbk. : alk. paper)
 I. Cumming, Robert B., 1928- II. Mobbs, Rebecca Passmore. III. Title.
 PS3537.C18U53 2011
 811'.54—dc22

2011027796

Acknowledgments

Grateful acknowlegment is made to the following publications where some of these poems first appeared, some in slightly different form:

Journals

American Poetry Monthly: "Preferment"
Buck & Wing:Southern Poetry at 2000: "The Garden"
Poetry: "Shi-te's New Year Prayer," "On the Third Anniversary Of Shi-te's Death," "The Dead," "The Traveler," "In Memoriam," "Han-shan Fashions A Myth," "Letter To Shi-te," "Music," "Preferment," "Up Front," "Early Schooling," "Catch-All," "Initial," "Revenant," "Anachronisms," "The Garden"
Shenandoah: "Commentary," "Endowment," "The Garden," "Lessons"
The Virginia Quarterly Review: "On the Third Anniversary of Shi-te's Death," "A Hole in a Cloud," "Compensation," "Night Out (Han-Shan at Eighty-two), "The Dead," "The Will-maker," "This Morning," "Rumor"
Zone 3: "Still Life"

Anthologies

Southern Voices in Every Direction: "Poems After Han-shan"
The Poetry Anthology 1912-2002: Ninety Years of America's Most Distinguished Verse Magazine: "Han-Shan Fashions A Myth"
The Southern Poetry Anthology (Vol. III): Contemporary Appalachia: " Singularity", Drouth", Monday", "Monday II", "Ancientry", "Dragonfly," "Roots"

Book

George Scarbrough, Appalachian Poet: A Biography and Literary Study with Unpublished Writings by Randy Mackin (MᴄFᴀʀʟᴀɴᴅ & Cᴏᴍᴘᴀɴʏ, Iɴᴄ. 2011) "Han-shan at Home," "Odd One In," "Upon Opening His Gifts on Christmas Eve," "Newscast," "Ministroke," "At Home," "Endowment," "The Invitation"

Internet

Chapter 16: (http://www.chapter16.org/content/last-festival) "At the Last Festival"

Many people have contributed to this project in ways both large and small, and we wish to express our thanks. All or parts of the manuscript were read by Judy Loest, Cathy Kodra, Beto Cumming, and John Lang, and their suggestions have greatly improved this book. Any errors that remain are the responsibility of the editors. We also wish to thank Randy Mackin, Mark A. Roberts, R. T. Smith, and Margaret Rogers for support throughout the project. And special thanks to Annie Armour and John Tilford of the Archives and Special Collections at the University of the South who have been strong supporters of all of the Scarbrough projects.

White clouds clinging to vague rocks.
Now I've lived here—how many years—

—Han-shan
translated by Gary Snyder

The Buddha forsook the joys of rank
because he pitied fools

—Shi-te
translated by Red Pine

CONTENTS

II

III

IV

Resonance Across Time and Cultures: An Introduction to George Scarbrough's Han-shan Poems

George Scarbrough was a very important but underappreciated voice in American poetry throughout the last half of the twentieth century. Born in 1915 into the emotional intensity and limiting circumstances of the hardscrabble sharecropper life of rural Polk County, Tennessee, he stood in stark contrast to those around him, both on his home ground and in the wider literary community. Blessed with exceptional intelligence and a prodigious memory, he was a keen observer of nature and of the social contradictions that surrounded him. He loved language throughout his long life, and he was strongly attracted to books and other writings. While growing up, he read everything he could get his hands on, including the many newspapers pasted onto walls to close the cracks and seal out the wind in the primitive tenant houses he cycled through as a child. He was the only one of the seven children of Oscar and Belle Scarbrough to graduate from high school.

Definition of "Home"

George Scarbrough was a consummate author of "place." In his preface to the second edition of *Tellico Blue* (Iris Press 1999), he says: "I am one of the few who never packed up their roots and left home…. After fifty years the mountains are still in place, still blue with distance, peaked and ridged, still rife with memory, still the habitation of wild boars, bears, deer and in the latter years re-stocked with the red wolf once plentiful in the region." For him "home" was a mental construct as much as a physical place. It was the mythical land he called "My Mesopotamia" or "Eastanalle," the wild land between the Hiwassee and Ocoee Rivers, that embodied for him everything that was of value in this world and everything that was evil. For him "Home" was all the memories of survival in a dying culture; it was the rich texture of being part of nature in an unspoiled place, and much more. It was part of him, and he couldn't have moved away from it if he had wanted to. But the definition of "home" is elusive and complex. How does one gain clarity about such a specific locality by reaching back over long periods of time to a very alien culture?

The one thing that George and his father seemed to agree on was that, as a child, George showed little aptitude for subsistence farming. But beneath the surface, away from the mule and plow and under the influence of his literate mother, he was framing a relationship with the living land that Oscar Scarbrough couldn't even dream of. In January of 1941, very early in George's career, Jesse Stuart, the Kentucky author who for a generation defined the relationship of humans to the rural Southern landscape, wrote to him: "You are an Agrarian in practice. You are truly an Agrarian. You are not an Agrarian of 'sweet theory,' not one who talks it and doesn't know anything about making a living from the soil. You are the true Agrarian who knows the earth, seedtime, growth and harvest. I hope you never lose this firm foundation." Thirty-five years later in 1976, after having read the manuscript for George's then impending fourth collection, *New and Selected Poems,* Allen Tate wrote: "In my opinion George Scarbrough is one of the few genuine poetic talents to appear in the South in the past generation. I hope that his work continues to get the attention it deserves." Nearly three years after his death Scarbrough's work continues to get attention, and his readership continues to grow.

A number of themes run through Scarbrough's life from his earliest days and emerge from time to time in both his published writings and in his copious journals. He cherished solitude but paradoxically was very sociable and loved to be with friends. He felt a deep, almost mystical relationship with nature and the land, and he loved to wander in wild places simply to observe animals and plants and put names on them. Awareness of death is a thread that runs through Scarbrough's entire body of work, and he experienced mortality often among cherished friends and relatives. Always conscious of time and its relentlessness, he had a well-developed sense of history and his place in it. There was a thread of humor that ran through much of George's writings and that frequently came out in his casual conversations. He was often brutally frank and honest but at the same time showed insecurity and concern about how others thought of him. He thus expressed firm opinions in elegant language and often displayed his many contradictions.

He also felt a pervasive sense of estrangement from many of his contemporaries and often believed they judged him harshly. This is particularly true of his relationship with his father, and it is apparent that the two men never fully understood each other. The main barrier was language, and for George and Oscar Scarbrough, facility with language could not have been more different. Oscar Scarbrough, a part Cherokee with little education, was at best semiliterate, and for him language was without subtlety, a blunt instrument often used as a weapon. For George language was rich and intricate, full of complexity and nuance, and capable of great beauty. And since language shapes each individual's understanding of the world, the father and son had mutually incomprehensible world views. George Scarbrough was concerned about sexual orientation issues throughout his entire life. He never dealt with these issues very explicitly in his writings until late in his life, but he clearly thought that they were a factor in his alienation from segments of society in his rural county, and certainly in the early years he was probably right. Sexual orientation also clearly played a part in his strained relationship with his father.

George Scarbrough wrote virtually every day for over sixty years, and in the process he accumulated a very large body of work, much of it still unpublished. This material is all destined to become a part of his archive at the University of the South at Sewanee, Tennessee, and a lot of it is already there. Most of it was written on his antique manual typewriter with thoroughly used ribbons and on any paper that he was able to salvage. George always needed a resourceful editor. I had the privilege of working with him, off and on, over the last twenty years of his productive life, and at the time I acquired Iris Press in 1996, all of his books that were still in print were with Iris. During that period, we discussed at length his plans and desires for further publications. Implementing his publication strategy proved to be more complicated and time consuming than we wished. The material was not well organized, often redundant with hand-written corrections, and none of it was initially in digital form. Editing for George has always been a labor-intensive exercise. But the publication plan is proceeding, much as George had envisioned it. Ultimately, most of George Scarbrough's past collections will be back in print, and there will be several collections of new material and in-depth critical studies.

INFLUENCES

Scarbrough read and wrote poetry from an early age. Since the intellectual environment in Polk County in the 1920s did not encourage or promote literary skills, the only way he could learn the craft was to read widely and to emulate the poems that he liked. He spent much of his life in the passionate search for resonant voices. The medium was always language: the sounds and rhythms and nuances. He approached his early and enduring love of nature through language, and it was language that set him apart from county friends and neighbors in his formative years. Language was largely the source of conflict with his father, whose speech, though colorful, was clumsy and imprecise, while George's precocious linguistic development allowed him to see the world through different eyes. Scarbrough read other poets copiously, always searching for works that resonated with his sensibilities, and he was quick to form judgments about the quality of those works.

When he found poems that he particularly liked, he would spend considerable time with them in an effort to determine the basis for their power. Analysis of his early work provides hints about what sorts of writing influenced him during his developmental period. Much of his earliest published work is in formal rhymed and metered verse, but his language was always too exuberant to be easily contained within rigid forms. Near the middle of his career the influences by earlier poets become more explicit. They began to show up, still a bit beneath the surface, in his third collection, *Summer So Called* (DUTTON 1956). In his first Iris Press collection, *New and Selected Poems* (1977), a poem appears entitled "After Baudelaire's

'The Albatross,' " and this is a harbinger of things to come. The "afters" started appearing with increasing frequency in his succeeding writings, in both his published works and in the vast trove of material in his archive.

In Scarbrough's fifth collection of poems, *Invitation to Kim* (Iris Press 1989), poems appear which are designated as "after" works by Seamus Heaney, Denise Levertov, William Carlos Williams, Jorge Luis Borges and Marco Antonio Campos, along with other influences that are not so explicitly labeled. In his later work, published and unpublished, are poems labeled "after" works by Wallace Stevens, Sylvia Plath and Federico Garcia Lorca, among others. George Scarbrough, clearly tuned in to the poetry world at large, knew what he liked and became passionate about it.

HAN-SHAN: LOVE AT FIRST SIGHT

Han-shan was a legendary eighth-century Chinese recluse, the most mysterious but least polished of the important T'ang Dynasty poets, and also the most resonant with many in the West. He called himself Han-shan, which literally translates into "Cold Mountain" in English. This was the name of the cave where he lived for many years at the foot of "Cold Cliff" in the Tenienti Mountains, a two-day walk from the East China Sea. The poet's real name is not known with certainty, and this was probably by design. Most likely a fugitive following the An Lu-shan rebellion of 755, he retreated at about the age of thirty to one of the most obscure locations in the empire and led a reclusive life, always dreaming of reconciliation. He often visited the Kuoching Temple, a long day's hike to the northeast, to visit his friends Shi-te (Pickup) and Feng-kan (Big Stick), who were also reclusive poets. The search for the historical Han-shan has always been a highly speculative and imprecise exercise, but there is some consensus among the important commentators on this poet's surviving work. A good summary of the speculations about the historical Han-shan appears in Red Pine's beautiful translation of all the known surviving Han-shan poems, *The Collected Songs of Cold Mountain* (Copper Canyon 2000).

There have been about ten important translations into English of various subsets of the over three hundred surviving Han-shan poems since Arthur Waley's translation of twenty-seven of them in 1954. Gary Snyder, perhaps the best known of these translators, published twenty-four of them in 1958, and was probably responsible for Han-shan being so warmly embraced by the beat generation writers. Jack Kerouac dedicated his novel, *The Dharma Bums,* to Han-shan at the suggestion of Snyder. Han-shan has been claimed by the Buddhists and the Taoists, and clearly he had a deep understanding of both religious traditions. But sharply critical of some aspects of both Buddhist and Taoist practice, he appeared to resist any challenges to his own opinions. Han-shan's poems are simple, direct and frank, never failing to call attention to the flaws in society as he sees them. They are a good model for people who feel alienated from society and wish to clearly but non-aggressively express their grievances. Perhaps this explains their appeal to the beat writers.

George Scarbrough was introduced to the Han-shan poems in the early 1990s in a 1962 translation by Burton Watson, and he recognized a kindred spirit. The reaction was immediate and enduring. He saw most of the themes that recur in his own writings, often in a veiled form, simply and clearly expressed in the Han-shan translations in Watson's little book. The rejection, isolation, solitude, desire for reconciliation, love of nature and the natural order, reaction to bigotry and corruption, and many other things were all there. George started writing about his ever present rural county concerns in the voice of an old recluse who lived in a cave half-way around the world thirteen hundred years ago and who addressed the abuses in Imperial China in clear and simple language. George entered one of the most productive periods of his writing life right at the end, and he never looked back.

The Uses of an Alter Ego

George Scarbrough had always been ambivalent about disclosing too much of his personal life for fear of being rejected by those whose good opinions he valued. He protected himself in his younger years by using intricate language as a code, feeling secure that many in his rural county would not be able to decipher his true meaning. In this way he covered up his liberal tendencies and homosexuality from people who were simply unable or unwilling to carefully read his published work. But language used this way has its limitations, and George knew it. His unwillingness to be fully open in his writings exacted a toll in productivity in the middle of his career, and much of his writing was funneled into his journals where he felt he could be more open. He felt he needed an alter ego to help him say the things he needed to say. George made it known in conversations that the Han-shan voice gave him the ability to address neglected issues in a clearer and more direct manner. In Randy Mackin's new book, *George Scarbrough, Appalachian Poet* (McFarland 2011), George is quoted in an interview:

> *He is my alter ego and I am finding that I can be, well perhaps, more truthful hiding behind Han-shan.... I am using him to cover a lot of things that are written under first person. I get so tired of "I." I get tired of "me," but I get tireder of "I." I love old Han-shan.... [He] has come in very handy. Han-shan, bless his old heart, has stood me in good stead.*

For some reason, George was more comfortable saying the things he felt compelled to express by attributing them to Han-shan than by stating them directly in his own voice.

Since the details of the life of the historic Han-shan are still obscure, this has allowed recent writers to imagine the kind of life for the old poet that suited their purposes. This was true of the beat generation writers who imagined Han-shan and Shi-te as outcasts in twentieth-century America. Snyder says of them: "They became immortals and sometimes you run into them today in the skidrows, orchards, hobo jungles and logging camps of America." Scarbrough imagined Han-shan and Shi-te in a loving, stable, homosexual relationship, and he felt free to do so because of the uncertainty about the details of the historic Han-shan's life.

Whatever the psychological basis for the use of an alter ego in writing about sensitive issues, it is clear that for George Scarbrough, the identification with Han-shan led to the most productive period of his writing career. At the time he started writing as Han-shan, George was declining physically and had only a few writing years left. In that short time, he produced about three hundred Han-shan poems in a burst of creativity. They were well received and a number of them appeared in prestigious journals. It was as if a barrier had been lifted. He could finally fully be himself by becoming someone else whose views on a number of issues he deeply respected. Han-shan gave him the means to speak directly and clearly about the social abuses and other problems he saw in his hyper-conservative home ground but never could address so clearly in his first-person voice. So he moved the old Chinese recluse to the land between the Hiwassee and the Ocoee Rivers in rural Polk County. The old sage has never seemed more at home. *Under the Lemon Tree* is a selection of 102 poems of the several hundred resulting from that translocation.

—Robert B. Cumming
Oak Ridge, Tennessee
September 2011

Prologue

At the Last Festival

"All things happy and true
Happen under the lemon tree,"
Han-shan remembers saying
To the young prince on
An April day when order and
Arrangement ruled the garden
And gnomes were still in style.

"Poetry originated in gardens,"
He had said, "among exotic trees
And flowers and the mazes
Of topiary art. Music's provenance
Had been among fountains, aided
And abetted by birdsong,
Wind chimes, and verbs that moved."

The armature of any garden,
However, he believes is words,
And he had sought to charm the boy
With the mysteries of philology,
Missaying in order to say, he said.
But words failed him now
At the sight of ruined imperial
Arcades and belle tournures.

Around him hedges were untrimmed,
And once exotic flowers allowed to go
Wild in unkempt corners.
No yellow bird sang above
The brackish pool where golden carp
Once glinted in the sun.
The lemon tree was gone.

Through the open door of what
Had once been his beloved house,
Merchants cried:
"Come buy! Come buy!
Oranges fresh from the country!
Melons from a far province!"

Settling himself among cushions
Of silk and figured leather, studying
His manuscripts, Han-shan began the journey
Home as if he had never been away.

I

Roots

Consciousness is the first hurt;
The word springs from the wound.
After that the first red flower;
And then the land itself, humid,
Intense with cedars, heavy with
Keen water and the purple smear
Of mountains and white stone's
Weight. The length of a meadow
Lays on a stripe, and the wind
Singing alone in weathered grasses.
But these are common hurts.
It is Love that denounces happiness, and
Friends who cast the first stone.
I write them this note of thanks.

PREDESTINATION

"All things come to little
In this over-estimated world,"
His mother declares,
Mixing breakfast batter.
"But one thing be denied:
Be he man or be he beast,
He who will dine must work."

Listening to her same-song,
Han-shan plaits and unplaits
His unemployed fingers,
Impatient with the slow plop
Of the great spoon turning
In the honied bowl, and telling
Himself, as he always does,
That he must take a trade.

But what trade will he take,
Or, better, what trade will take him?
Inept at weaving, too short-sighted
For embroidery and other cottage
Industry, awkward even at combing
His own hair, he is unable
To beat the air without
Breaking his arm, his father says.
Given the football, he runs
The wrong way and scores
For the other team.

Plowing is past his power.
Wood-chopping impossible.

What, then, will he do:
Paint ladyfingers at festivals?

Between their altercations,
Sell rice cakes to lawyers
On Circuit-court day?
Hunt through the trees for dainties
To please a merchant's palate:
Grabble for groundnuts,
Truckle or truffles?
Drive dilatory geese to market?

Net Butterflies for sedentary Lepidopterists?
Count skylarks in season
For bearded statisticians
Opportunities seem endless:

"But I'll not work at any
Of these things," he mutters
To himself, his mouth watering,
Hearing the great spoon scrape
The side of the breakfast bowl
 "I'd rather make a wooden beak
And peck dung with the chickens.
I was meant to be a poet,
And a poet I will be:

Tuning flutes at festivals,
Leading dances at celebrations,
Being acclaimed for my elegant
Bon mots and delectable phrases,
Measuring iambs not shoes
For distance rickshaw runners.

And I'll be doubly damned if
I catch pennies at toll-gates
To build another highway,
Even if I do grow spatulate
Thumbs from sopping sweet platters

In my dear mother's kitchen
While waiting for the dumb-ass
Editor of the Rump County News
To say that a good time was had
By all who came to the party

And print my matchless haiku
Among the want ads
Of this weekly edition.

ODD ONE IN

My father called me Kai-te's boy,
And I was glad to be so identified,
Being too much like her not to be.

When he spoke of me to others
There was a note of caution in his voice.
But I grew to fill his house.

Cowbird in cuckoo's nest,
Dislodging all the others,
Until I became the oldest child

In the county. It was clear
That I had become famous for
My juvenile delinquency.

Even my mother looked ashamed
When her other children came home
And asked about their famous brother.

"He's somewhere about reading a book,"
My father said. "He's somewhere about
Looking for stolen nests," my mother opined.

"The cat has shat in the flax,"
My elder brother said. "You'll never
Get him off your hands."

I went to all the funerals.
I avoided all the churches.
Stayed out of all processions.

I always stayed at home,
Or walked my father's fields
alone.

Now I live where I was born,
Liege lord of all I survey
By right of occupancy.

MONDAY

Han-shan loved churning day—
the bashing clashing dashing lashing
mashing smashing nattering battering
pattering spattering splattering
neaping leaping sweeping heaping
backing hacking tacking quacking
tracking cracking packing slacking
racking pounding sounds rounding
grounding founding flavoring savoring
clavering favoring wavering muttering
spluttering uttering buttering—
the whole messy mattering—

while his mother wove
another sort of magic at the stove:
Bread making
Always set his teeth aching,
His legs quaking,
And his back breaking
Han-shan thought he would smother.

He adored his mother
And his mother adored Han-shan:
That is, as much as a mother can,
Running between stove and churn
As loving mothers will,
Lest something spill
Or something burn.

After what seemed an eternity
Of dash and commotion,
What they looked in to see
Floating on a calm ocean

In the summer sun
Was the golden islet of Hesperide.

And the golden bread was done.

Monday II

Han's mother taught him what her
Own mother had taught her: to sand
A floor for scouring but to disdain
The crunch underfoot.

Old preachments keep surfacing.
Han goes for the grain in the wood,
Strings the nerve of board and vein
To bare exhilaration,

Scrubs his own pits raw,
Scumbles stench with lavender.
Yet he has not attained the godliness
She subscribed to,

No, not in time enough
To have entered the trinity
As a rinsing mist among those
Landmark stars.

CHRISTMAS MORNING

Han-shan smiles at the young cat
Snarled in the yarns of holiday,
And his heart is seized with tears.

What can bright strings avail against loss?
What advantages accrue from the prodigy
Of the new calf born in the midst of snow?

The calf nuzzles his hand
And gallops around in the warm stall
While the mother moos soft animal

Music for her son to dance by.
The old brown mare hangs her head over
The half-door to nuzzle the new born.

The barn is snug with left-over clover,
Taut with thyme left over from summer
The cat is a raveling stringball.

But what, Han-shan wonders, have these
Loved and lovely things to do
With the other bitter love?

Spring Freshet

Eating an onion sandwich, Han-shan
Delights in the quiet, spring rain,
Remembering the Year of the Great Flood
When his garden floated past the front door
And he fished for his dinner from the step-
Stone while his only rooster, Red Peony,
Sailed away to the sea on a rainbarrel
And never came home again.
That year he had spoken ill of the raingod.

INSPIRATION

Han-shan never knows what he will
Write when he gets up in the morning:
In his heathenish way, he thinks
Of divine afflatus as a capricious bird
Flying over his sheet of white rice
Paper, dropping what it may:
Sometimes a gauzy feather, sometimes
A splatter of mulberry shit. Fruit
Time is a good time for colorful poems,
Especially of the latter sort. "Let
Fall what will," the old poet says as he
Takes up his quill.
"It's all the same in the end."

AT HOME

Before going into the village,
Han-shan washes and mends
His good, gray clothes
To wear among the citizenry,
Liking to think himself invisible
Against the weathered walls
As a monk girded in the drabness
Of his faith.

Home again, in his garden,
He goes pantless among his rows:
Below his belted shirt, his brown
Legs become balletic. Under
A pavilion-wide hat, weeding leeks,
Melons, and sunflowers, he has all
The aspects of an ambulatory toadstool.
He is a different man.

Indoors, he draws all curtains,
Scours himself with aromatic rushes,
Rubs down with imported oils,
And, wearing an embroidered garnet gown,
Moves along the shelves of prized volumes
Before he returns to the old story
Of a foreign boy who dared to go
Among his hostile brothers
Drest in a coat of costly
Divisive colors.

SINGULARITY

Because he had been one of nine
In his father's house, Han-shan
Has never been able to use plurality
Wisely. "One man makes a poor team,"
His father opined. But the son
Had dissented. Consequently Han had
Not lived easily in the plural world.
"I'm a man of sense not census,"
He says grimly. Dismissed early
From the capital because of his
Singularity, he had come here.
Remembering his father's house as
He walks under the trees on Exile
Mountain, "A whole plantation," he says,
"Is beautiful and good to see,
But a solitary pine jutting out
From a headland is also fair
And commendable."

THE CENSUS-TAKER

As he makes his way along the lane,
Han-shan uses his staff as pointer,
Taking count of his neighbors,
Establishing points of reference:

In that house lives a young man
With eyes as red as a grandmother's
Ringstone, hair like milkweed down,
And a purple blaze on one side
Of an otherwise fair face:

"One albino, male, with birthmark,"
Han-shan states on his civic page.

Behind the adjoining house, a wash
Of brilliant smocks and sashes
Hangs to dry in the morning sun.
What an astonishing array it is!
Han has heard much of this man:

"One male cross-dresser of
Excellent taste," he records.

Across from the man with many colors,
Two women hold hands in a doorway.
Each has one eye of another color.
Together, they compose two pairs
Of eyes of the same color:

"Two lovely anomalies of visual
Imperfection," Han notes
In his expanding catalogue.

A doorway down from the lustrous
Duet, a small brown man babbles
A county Spanish no one understands
When he talks to himself
He keeps a blue-and-gold parrot
Who speaks Portuguese:

"One total nonesuch," Han-shan reports,
"Plus his feathered henchman."

Next to the house of tongues
Sojourns the man slim and tall
As a blue pine in scrub timber.
When he smiles, a silver tooth
Illumines the darkness of his face.
He is black and resplendent
As a walking lighted tower:

"One sight to see," Han-shan posts
In his thriving journal.

At the next bend in the lane is the seat
Of the local magistrate, who plants
Bold dahlias in his yard one year
And small pale chicories another,
Stooping among his rows in a damask
Robe printed with bellflowers and stars:

"One judge who likes pansies,"
Han-shan pencils with a flourish.

Last in the count is the house
Of the proclaimed angel who holds
Veiled soirees with darkened lamps
And tramontane incense and ointment.
Han-shan feels an affinity with

The transplanted celestial, whom
He would like to know better, but so
Far has not learned her name.
Behind a masque of fleurs-de-lis,
She remains a very discreet person:

"One carnival queen," Han-shan adds
To his finished chronicle.

But what, he asks himself,
Of the meter-man, who wears a torn
Yarmulke and speaks of purification?
Or of the postman who comes
From the province of Znejiang,
Heaps coils of lapis lazuli
On sallow off-hand fingers,
And says nothing at all?

"I must remember to ask when we meet,"
Han-shan reminds himself; turning home.

Back in his own house, feet up,
Han-shan reads over his memoranda.
He is delighted with what he reads.
"I'll send *them* numbers instead,"
He says. "This is much too beautiful
To waste away in the archives
Of an insincere government."

BAMBOO

Han-shan is suffering a consequence:
He has been excluded from the capital
Because of a poem he wrote in admission
Of himself, saying thus and so:
A matter purely of identification
Beyond the usual number in a census,
Which does not include an admiration
Of the young Prince's hands. Ah, those
Thin hands dripping with ivory rings!
For this, he has been banished here
To Exile Mountain, among dark pines and early snows
That turn trees overnight whiter
Than his own white head. "This follows
Upon that," he advises himself; listening
To the wind howl over the lip of the crag.
"And all because a young hand lifted in salute
To an old poet who wrote haiku on occasion
For the Emperor's entertainment."
The Emperor had not been entertained.
Intrigue had lifted its always *unsleeping* head.
The prince was involved. Allotments
Were cut, sinecures withdrawn.
On Exile Mountain, Han-shan addresses
The matter of consequence, matching effect
With cause…. "Moment of moonlight,"
He writes. "A fine hand lifted—
Motion of bamboo."

ACKNOWLEDGEMENT

Without the tall blue pine outside
The window, the river rounding the point
Of a spur of Exile Mountain, and the white
Capital distantly shining like an okra
Blossom in the sun, Han-shan admits he would
Be much lonelier. "But I must not discount
The chipmunk nor belittle the doorstone
Hollyhock nor defame the cucumber vine at
The front gate," he reminds himself.
"Besides, there is the handsome postman
To read my poems. He must have a melon
Today. Yet he is much like the young prince.
I must be careful, when he hands me a letter,
Not to caress those slim brown fingers."

POLITICS

How clamorous the henyard:
What bustle and industry,
What queuing and cliquing!
Looking out, Han-shan remembers
The faraway capital in April:
From the grand vizier down
To the pink-faced pages.
How handsome they were!
He recalls the year he was
Freshman senator, inexperienced
As a page. Indeed, he had once
Been taken for one. How like a young
Cockerel he had been, unfledged,
Bound to show his ass as indeed,
He had done. What had he known
Of rights, female or gay? He
Hardly knew his street address
When he cast his first ballot.
But he had learned to dissemble,
How to wear his coat just so.
"It is better," he opines now
To the dragonfly on the sunflower,
"To have an honest rump than to wear
An expensive coat," as he had done
Only too well. "How soon the cockerel
Becomes the cock!" he exclaims,
Listening to the quatter of his flock,
Here on Exile Mountain where he has
Been retired on half a pension.
It pains him to reminisce. But he
Laughs when his golden rooster,
Announcing his Great Plan to Reform
The Henyard, loses his foothold on
The fence and topples backward,
Doing unexpected cartwheels.

OF POETRY

Han-shan is a connoisseur
Of words. After all, he used to be
Head honcho down at the busy capital
In the good old days of poetry.
Now, here on Exile Mountain,
Gathering fiddlehead ferns
He explains to Mr. Salamander
How it was there in town,
From the loveliest stilted phrase
To the commonest expression.

DISMISSAL

After Han-shan had left the capital
Under suspicious circumstance,
Which he refused to make explicit,
And his brothers had come inquiring
To Exile Mountain, he gave them
Fresh morels on beds of young cabbage
Leaves but no explanation. He gave them
Clear spring water and sweet wormless
Chestnuts for dessert but no explanation.
When they left at dusk, eyeing him askance
Where he leaned on the garden gate,
Insects had begun their queer, local song
In the tulip poplar trees.

News from the Capital

Dismissed from his employment
For sins of love, Han–shan determines
To keep to his house on Exile Mountain
And forget the interfering world.
For awhile this goes well. Then a doubt
Begins to trouble him. Now he goes
Each day to sit on the cliff's edge
High above the valley and look far
Out and down on the white capital
In its maze of yellow roads, in search
Of a familiar figure in a coat he knows.
"If I forget the world," he tells himself,
"I will be forgotten." And by the next
Traveler to cross the mountain on the way
To town, he sends a letter to the young
Prince, praising the delicate ringed fingers
He had often kissed before the Emperor knew.

CONNIVANCE

When his garden vines began
To flourish in the roadway,
Han-shan recognized a sly
Potential for good:

The royal courier might lose
His footing there and fall,
Thus squashing the squashes
And so befouling himself

The owner of the property
Would be summoned to town
To stand trial for his
Egregious incaution.

In court, Han-shan declares,
I'll read my latest poem aloud
Before the bailiff can stop me,
And so charm the Emperor

I'll be asked back
To my old post as laureate
To the crown. Ah, how good
It will be to walk again

With the young Prince
In the Imperial Garden,
Under ricebirds singing
In the lemon trees.

And how happy I will be
To see my poems displayed
Along the Royal Route to town
And have them pointed out

To passers-by!
What triumph, what blissful
Justification! What! What!
But no such luck transpires.

When the courier arrives,
He skips blithely over
The wandering vegetables
And falls flat on his face among

The cabbages of another man's
Plantation, leaving Han-shan
To consider the vagarious ironies
Of courtly love

And what he could plant
To greater advantage
In his garden next year.

IGNIS FATUUS

From his house on Exile Mountain,
De-commissioned and dismissed from
The capital, Han-shan looks down on
A vast tract of trembling earth
That lies between him and the city.
Green willow grows there, and sweet
Calamus, whose roots are signatured
To many uses. Han had come that way
Here. From his aerie he can see on
Certain nights globes and strakes
Of light hissing up from the swamp
And reminding him of carnival in the city
Where poems are recited and celebrated.
Once he had read his own poems
In the Public Square: to bursting music,
Soaring illumination, and the people's
Thunderous approval. How admired
And happy he had been! Now when lights
Rove, he reads a poem at the cliff's
Raw edge to the sound of howling wind,
Imaging a carnival has learned of
His whereabouts and come to applaud him.

ENDOWMENT

Han-shan is not indifferent to fame.
Often he imagines himself winner
Of the literary competition held each
Year at the capital, to which end
He stores his poems in the family's
Ivory ringbox, ready for transport
Should the invitation come.

Ah, he thinks, at fall festival to stand
Among the great bards of the province!

What troubles him is that he has no robe
Fit to wear in such company nor any way
To arrive at the august presentation
Except on foot. No one he knows
Owns a mule he might borrow
For a trip to town.

Then there are those scandalous reports
He hears of what the judges demand
For a favorable decision.
A coupling for a couplet!
What, Han-shan wonders, would a villanelle
Cost him by way of quittance.

Each year, on the night of funding,
He sits at the crag's lip reading his pieces
Toward town in his loudest voice,
But no runner comes upmountain
To announce the good news.

So he adds another season's worth
Of poems to his already brimming box
And plants another garden in the purlieus
Of summer, telling himself that in all reason
He should have been a ringmaker
Like his father.

POETRY FESTIVAL

Tossing grain to his crowing hens
And cackling cocks, Han-shan
Remembers with regret.

Being forbidden to return
To the capital had been a bitter blow.

"At this very moment," he tells
His flock, "My rivals are reading
Their poems in the Great Pavilion
To plaudits that last year were mine,
And I am at home, feeding you noisy fools.

What is worse, the Emperor is coming
Here for a day of entertainment
On Exile Mountain.

Ah, those bony fingers
Furnished with rondues of lapis lazuli
And those withered wrists ringed with
Carven ivory cold as stone.

Boys tell all they know
And are not to be trusted.
Old men are crafty.

How could I have forgotten this
When I strolled with the young prince
In moonlight and kissed the smooth
Warm hand in the shadow of bamboo?
O that I had bitten my impassioned
Tongue instead of speaking
The offensive word!"

RECONCILIATION

Han-shan, the Emperor's poet,
Once composed an ode to the young
Prince's hands and unwisely sang
It in public (ah, those slim white
Fingers strung with bands of stammel,
Ebony, and gold: how utterly charming
They had been!) Now, as penalty,
The old poet lives alone on Exile
Mountain: stay-at-home forbidden
To travel, tending his fragrant melon
Patch and orchard of apple trees.
But a maze of roads spreads out from
The capital. "One day," Han-shan
Consoles himself, "the Emperor's son
Will find his way to my door, and I
Will be able to kiss my lord's fingers
Once again. Meanwhile, I can be
Reasonably happy with house and land,
Not misprizing the chipmunk nor
Belittling the red hollyhock by
The doorstone nor disesteeming
The blue lentil at the gate."

No News

Han-shan longs to hear again
From the lips of state officials
What is happening at the capital:

Details of the ailing Emperor's health;
What the young prince wore at the last
Banquet for foreign emissaries;
Whom (and for what) the lord lieutenant
Has lately detained, and what judgment
The trembling wretch received
For his enormous crime

But most of all he wants to know
Who is beadle now in his old place.
How proudly he had led the processions!

Travelers who cross Exile Mountain
Know nothing of such important things:
For a cup of water, they exchange only
The idiocy of the local news.

RETROSPECT

Without women to wile me, Han-shan,
Without liquor to make me laugh at the moon,
What profit to have remained there
Between plow handles on a county hill?
What was there besides the railroad track
That never stopped running?
Threading brambles and old woods
I went seeking what books promised.
Now I have no plow to follow
Along such furrows as I never dreamed of.
What profit to have come here if what
I own is only a passel of books
Too bundlesome to fit a good, gray mule's back
When I tire of my landlord?

II

SHI-TE'S NEW YEAR PRAYER

Lord of all patches and gardens
And rows taking root under
Beneficent eaves, let not the savors
Of paradise be too sudden,
Lest we be drowned in gulfs
And landslides of manifold sweetness.

Rather, allow us to relish first-
Turned dewberries still on the edge
Of unripeness, stony figs,
Downy crabapples, sour sallets
To modify the untempered
Dulcitudes of Heaven.

Han-shan Apologizes to Himself and to the World

It is true that certain double-mindedness
Has caused my parents to make
Unexpected journeys to strange
Houses along unmapped roads
And present me to bearded officials
Who sniffed me as though I were

A ripe garden melon, lifting
My best robe and touching me here
And there with warm, suspicious hands!
And O those locative fingerpost
Pointing both ways in uneasy wind
And orchards of irrelative apples

Of foreign distinction falling
On the brink of nameless rivers....
(We have not gone there recently:
In careful families mutants,
like Apples are often confirmed
To assure ancestral progress.)

Come visit me in my small
Prefabricated house in a faded
Government suburb where, among
Radish beds and sweet lettuces,
Apples and peaches and cherries,
Cosmos, windflowers, hollyhocks,

And rock roses, I wear old shoes
And the fabulous gold ring of antique
Fashion he gave me long ago,
And sit daily picking out on this old
Upright Remington my marginal
But hospitable poems.

In the dust of the yard once
Satined with delicate grasses,
Young boys tumbled about like headless
Fowl in the environs of inns.

Thinking of what he would have
To tell Shi-te, sick at heart,
Han-shan walked on, listening for
Birdsong, for water tinkling
In fountains, for wind sweeping
Through feathery pecan trees.

In one place, inquiring
Of the Emperor, Han-shan was advised
To ask among the men shouting around
A gaming table and was informed there
By a tall, courtly man who eyed him
Coldly and who might have been
The Emperor himself, that on feast days
The Prime Minister discharged
All imperial obligations.

Walking wearily away, Han-shan
Looked back to see his informant,
Still staring, salute him
With a covert flick of the hand.

At a shoemaker's shop, Han-shan asked
Where he might find a place
To bathe and rest.
"I've traveled far," he said.
The keeper was annoyed. Prospective
Customers were passing him by.
"Wash in the fishpond," he counseled.
"Make your bed on the ground
As others are doing.
I've a living to make."

HAN-SHAN AT HOME

Han-shan likes coziness.
His house is small, even as small houses go.
He raises a window without getting out of bed,
And from his chair, stirs a fire on the hearth.
But it is his kitchen that is so snugly convenient.
There, he stands in the middle of the floor
And spins like a lazy susan doing both
His cooking and his serving.
A little man in a small house living
A large life, is how he views himself.
When he gets dizzy turning his cakes,
He blames his giddiness on his ears.

AFTER SUPPER

Above the purple mountain
Horizontal cloud-streaks
Stack like pantry shelves
On which nothing but a slice
Of melon remains.
Seeing them, Han-shan laughs aloud,
They are so like his own kitchen,
With its one polished brass pan.

Neighbors

Han–shan interrogates Mr. Crow:
"Sir," he says, "why do you find it
Necessary to strike so hard?
Even the bones I toss you
Leap back from your hammerblows.
Are you trying to reinvest the dead?

Once you belabored a burned pot-pie
Around the house and back again
Without making a dint.
Do you know nothing of resilience
And the law of compensation?
Does your head not ache from diligence?
Frankly, Sir, have you been to school?

Further, Sir, why do you persist
In keeping one eye on the sky?
Does the corvine esthetic allow
A taste for the cerulean?
Or, as some vulgarians do,
Do you only pretend an admiration?
Or could it be that you, Sir,
Also believe in God?"

DRAGONFLY

Last night I dropped my famous
Crystal cup into the spring.
This morning it is nowhere to be seen.
I've dazzled my eyes with looking.
My knees ache from the kneelingstone.
Even on my table it was invisible,
Empty until shaken, so great was
The clarity of what it held.
Only a dragonfly with isinglass
Wings, and sand grains spinning
Now make a little something of the light.

GRACE

On days when Shi-te does not go
To work at the quarry,
Merriment begins at the doorway.

At mid-day, over yellow bowls
Of emerald soup, Han-shan and his friend
Are still laughing:

How elusive the young peas were
Among the tropic vines! And how the Devil
Jumped out at Shi-te, causing him
To step back and lose his balance!

"Mr. Mantis," Han-shan says,
Saying grace,
"Keep preying among the lentils."

ABSENCE

When Shi-te goes into town,
Han-shan keeps company with the man
In the mirror.

"You," he says, "are a nonesuch:
Lending your only good shirt
To a passer-by and sharing your
Supper crust with a fellow-traveler.

Yet, if you *lose* a chipped marble
In the grass, you are troubled for days.
You mourn the board dropped from
The ceiling and grieve for the nail
Fallen out of its socket
In the wall:
You comb the grass incessantly."

Han-shan lectures the man in the glass:
"What you want," he says accusingly,
"Is a childish sense of continuity:
Series that go on and on without
Interruption: blessed assurance:
A concourse of constancy."

The man in the mirror drops his eyes
And turns away from the accusation.

On his writing stand,
A shard of yellow jade weights
A stack of clean rice paper.
His writing brushes are dry.

From his station on the high cliff,
Han-shan looks far along the road
That leads to the capital:
An owl cries in the mountain.

Shi-te has been gone too long.

First Frost

Through the window, Han-shan
Regards the vegetable garden,
Drawn by the phallic image
Of ruined pepperpods.

Yesterday, Shi-te, pleading
Homesickness, returned
To his own cold-water county.
At mid morning, Han-shan

Is still playing arpeggios
On the keys of his stalled typewriter
And waiting for a change back to blue
Of the valley's suddenly sullen weather.

LETTER TO SHI-TE

"Just now when I, Han-shan, said your name,
A green heron rose from the White River
And flew off toward the state line.

You called 'Goodbye' last night,
Looking back to where I stood
Among catkined willows.

How swiftly darkness came.
Now what does it matter
That the man walking toward me on the road

Is the handsomest of men
Or so ugly as to make the gods laugh?
Who sees after dark?

The dint of your dark head
On the pillow of the other bed
Holds the spill of my unwept tears.

Here is part of the problem.
You will be gone until spring.
Wild ducks at the river will starve

Without the seedcakes we tossed them."

THE LETTER

My Dear Shi–te, I miss you grievously.
This is only one of the many letters
I've written to you this winter.
The old rush basket by the door
Is filling up with uncollected bulletins
Awaiting the postman to come by.

Since the first great snowfall
That came early this season, no climber
Has dared the head–high drifts that bar
Access to Exile Mountain.
The cold is excessive. My hands are numb
And stiff as I write what I cannot read
Myself. I soak them for hours in warm water.
But it does no good. Hens make better
Scratchings in the snow. Around me, trees
Rise like black script from a white page.

The snow falls even when it isn't falling.
Blown about when the wind thrashes, it flies
All day. The hens huddle under the porch
Floor and complain, as if they blame me
For this outrage of weather. They are all
The company I have. The wood we cut in October
Is holding out, and the rice bin is at
The right seasonal level. I'm warm and well
Fed and reasonably clean with plenty of water
From the eaves. Cleanliness is some comfort,
Although the bed is cold at night.

A new man moved in from the capital
Just before winter struck with full force.
I've not seen the new–comer as yet,
But it is rumored that he is a distant man

And does not speak even when spoken to.
That I can believe. I remember that during
My first year on the Mountain, I declined
All offers of human companionship.

No one knows why the new-comer was sent up.
Some crime against imperial pretension,
Presumably. Do you remember the case
Of the poor fellow who was arrested and
Transported for bathing with the young Prince
In the palace garden and stealing fruit
From the Emperor's lemon tree: two misdemeanors
Made into one? And how severe the sentence!
What a stir in the great hall among
The rancorous politicians, some of whom
Were the Prince's suitors and should have
Been deployed among the coldest summits.

Perhaps the stranger did not light the royal pipe
With proper flare, or made an egregious error
In transcribing an imperial text, thus causing
The Emperor embarrassment, which no one does
With impunity. I wonder what the errant
Word might have been that brought the scribe's
Dismissal. In any event, he lives here now
In a house I can see on a clear day.

It is said that he spends his time bent
Over scraps of old rice paper, scrupulously
Computing profiles that look remarkably
Like the faces we all would know:
That of the bailiff who hailed us into court,
Of the clerk who reads out the charges,
And of the judge whose verdict always silences
The courtroom. It is said that he sticks
Pins in all the justicial eyes.

My hands are tired and sore from the effort
Of writing. I must go and hold my swollen
Fingers in a pan of warm water.
I miss you, old friend. Come home at first
Snow-melt and tell me all the news.

HOMECOMING

In Han–shan's house,
Basking his feet in warm water,
Shi–te explains to his host,
"Though guilty only by association,
I left town the day you were remanded
To exile on this mountain
For dallying with the young prince
Under the lemon trees.

No one tried to hinder me.
The gate was wide open.
One guard waved farewell.
Another saluted as I walked past.
You know their names.

Beset by wild dogs that inhabit there,
Sleeping in trees to forefend them,
I traveled far in strange lands,
Often in ruined sandals
On sockless feet.
Now and again I tarried with kind men
Who took me into their houses
And wept when I went.

I still dream of mad eyes glaring upward,
And of those other eyes pleading,
Stung with tears.
But one cannot remain young forever,
And unwise.

My insteps no longer arched
Like bridges in lands of flowers;
My once fine ankles streaked with blue.
My fat calves were no longer fit
For the escutcheons one sometimes finds
In barbershops of classic ideality.

Gone were the choice words,
The easy smile for strangers."

Han- Shan interrupts Shi-te's progression.
"I can know little of what you tell,
Shi-te, though I doubt none of it,"
He says, pouring more warm water
Into the tub for Shi-te's sore feet.

"You are a fortunate man.
Tonight, you will sleep in a clean bed
And dream to the sound of wind soughing
In our own pine trees, secure as
A roach leaning against the lee side
Of a transverse river stone,
Out of harm's way.

It is as if we never parted.
Put on your new shoes, my good friend,
And let us hie to a brook I know
Hidden away among mountain willows
And bring home ferns and water sallet
And a string of April fishes
For the reception dinner."

HOMECOMING II

Han-shan reaches across
The basket of garden peas
They are shelling between
Them and strokes
His old friend's hand.

"I am a fool, Shi-te," he says,
To go wandering." Not answering
At once, Shi-te leans forward
And tugs Han-shan's beard
As if tolling a bell.

Han-shan expands his remorse:
"Turn back the clock," he says.
"Reverse the calendar.
Nothing is retrieved:
The sand keeps pouring

In the glass of time."
A cuckoo calls from the top
Of the blue pine tree.
The pale lemon moon
Quarters the evening sky.

"How fat these legumes are!"
Shi-te says, laughing slyly.
"One might string them like beads.
There's a poem somewhere
Hereabout, Han-shan."

BACK HOME

Han-shan reaches across the basket
Of fresh peas they are shelling
And strokes his friend's hand:
"I was a fool, Shi-te," he says.
"A man's expectancy should never
Exceed his knowing.
I never suspected. I never knew."

Shi-te, not answering at once,
Tugs at his friend's chin-beard
As if he were tolling a bell.
Han-shan expands his remorse:
"Turn back the clock," he says,
"Reverse the calendar,
And nothing is won."

A cuckoo calls from the top
Of the tall, blue pine tree upmountain.
The sun, more golden than lemons,
Is quartering the morning sky.
"How round and fat these legumes
Are! There is a poem somewhere
Hereabout, Han-shan,"
Shi-te says, laughing.

To Whom It May Concern

"Dearly beloved," Han-shan writes
In his day-book, "let it be known
That I am not a man of greatly
Expanded preferences.

Take the matter of dress.
Growing up, I had but two shirts
And one change of trousers to my name,
Of sheerest simplicity and sparely
Cut and sewn by my mother.

Into and out of the wash
They lasted but a short while.
The same routine still holds,
Though blue is not a chosen color.

I had no hat to shield me
When I worked in the fields
Or picked hedgerows for berries,
Except my mother's slat bonnet,
Its strings tied under my chin.

How the plowmen laughed
Seeing me steal from vine to vine
To escape their derision.
What amorous words they spoke,
Fondling themselves in offering,
Doffing their own headgear.

I have two hats now, one yellow,
One green, to wear about.
Likewise, two suits of trousers,
Differently dyed, and two shirts
Of different predilections.

On ordinary days, I mix colors
To astonish the crows.
On other days, however I go drest
Head to foot in matched complexions
In deference to my mother's
Bleeding fingers."

ANACHRONISMS

In memory of John Crowe Ransom

Visitors arrive at Han–shan's house
Exclaiming the distances they've traveled
To reach his address and of how
The chairboys' feet bled on the way.

They found him, they say, in cyberspace,
A mode of discovery the old man knows
Nothing about. He offers wine and gives each
Of his guests a poem on fine rice paper,

Which they fold and put away in carryalls,
Still talking of distance and wonders
Of modern science, ignoring the credentials
Han has framed and hung about in easily

Observable places. After they are gone,
Still talking and waving back to him,
The good agrarian poet drinks tea from
His blue cup and stands at the South

Window, sniffing the scent of warm
Roses wafted from beyond the plantation
Of pecan trees edging the bottom
Of his herb garden.

Remonstrance

You complain, Mr. Chen,
That my poems are left unfinished.
I applaud your percipience.
My poems *are* unfinished.
I have not, however,
Abandoned them.

I would remind you, Master,
Sometimes the last line
Appears years later
When, and only when
You have forgotten
The poem is yours.

Last Will and Testament

Ancient Han-shan is becoming
Verifiably disjunctive, as Shi-te
At times laughingly reminds him:
Every day, he rewrites his last
Poem and hides it away
In the toe of an old boot,
To be found later, when the time comes,
By whoever cares to examine an old shoe,
Especially an unmatched one.

On some days, Han rewrites a new
Last poem which is essentially
The same last poem he had stashed away
The day before. The poem, like all
The other poems, an epitaph,
Is a very short poem. So far,
He hasn't changed his shoe.
Shi-te, himself not so exalté,
Observes and smiles.

Sometimes, Han wears the last version
Behind the peacock feather in his hatband,
Before putting the precious bond away.
O yes! He has still, on occasion,
A dapper day—feels cocky still
With a little exertion.
Whimsically, Shi-te thinks:
"How will it be when all his poems
Cleave together to make a new single-
Footed sole for an old lover to walk on?"

In Memoriam for Shi-te

Remembering Shi-te's counsel
Always to sit to a good table
And be joyous over wine
Among trusted friends,
Han-shan goes now wherever
Men practice being men.

Among his itineraries,
He hies best the annual
Sharpening of knives:
The whine of good steel
Laid against wet whetstones,
Waterdrops flung into high air,
And the edged blades turned
Out in interjacent rows
Upon the new grass.

"Soon,"
He says, "farthest corners
Of fields will be trimmed
To manly precision, bared
Footpaths will run like naked
Veins on sleeveless forearms,
And once-veiled islands will rise
Like headlands in leveled seas."

Thinking of what is to come,
He hears an unassignable music,
Small as wind, blowing among
Lemon trees in Imperial gardens.

Frequenting the mule markets,
He assesses the merits
Of each beast without pricing one.
The long ears please him,
The look of patient wisdom:
Anomaly among anomalous kingdoms.

THE DEAD

For James Joyce

How quickly Han-shan has forgotten
His address. The street is the right
Street, running along the hillside,
But where among the huddled houses
Of the government suburb
Is the one he calls home?

Snow has begun to fall.
"White houses," Han-shan reflects,
"Lose their identity in general
Albescence."

Even the serrated peaks
That compose the Mountain
Are growing nameless now
In the democracy of snow.

"Where in all that generality
Is Littlejohn Knob?" Han-shan wonders.
He inquires direction of a man
Who waits, shovel at rest
For the increase of tumbling flakes.

The stranger answers question
With question. "How long have you
Lived here?" he asks.
"Isn't this a bit too early for snow?"

Angrily, Han-shan thinks,
"We're two old ronyons playing
At non-sequiturs in a snowstorm."
But he answers civilly:
"In a new country, one learns

To temper the wind to the shorn lamb,"
Hardly knowing what his grandmother
Had meant, he is so cold.

Thanking the stranger for what
Information has passed between them,
Han-shan plods on, upslope, downslope.
Where, in all that whiteness
Is his little white house
With its swept porch and yellow
Summer chairs, object of amusement
To his remarking neighbors?

Where is the ancient tulip tree
In the front yard? Where, behind
The saffron door, are the warm
Book-lined room and the picture
Of Shi-te as a young man? Where
The bronzed Greek youths hurling
Discuses from the fireboard?

Tiring, he eases himself
Groundward by the roadside, resting
His head on his bent knees, and waits.
Some passerby would surely find him there
And guide him upmountain before dark.

Everywhere about him, in silver
And dark flakes, the snow is falling
On the road, on the rocks, on the trees:
All the sceneries of familiar earth,
Making them strange and untenable.

Snow is falling too on the lonely
Hill where Shi-te lies buried.
Han-shan hears the snow falling faintly
Throughout the universe.

INTERIMS

Han-shan seldom drinks
From his grandmother's prized
Blue and Gold cup:
Birthdays, graduations, publication
Of another thin book of poems:
Otherwise, it sits on the shelf
Above the small wall mirror.

On The Third Anniversary of Shi-te's Death

The Analects declare it is best
To withdraw from one's generation.
Next, to withdraw to another land.
Next, to leave because of a look.
Next best, to leave because of a word.

All of these advisements had applied
But none directly to Han-shan's reason
For departing the capital.
Option was the least of it.

A kiss taken from the high
Cheek of the youngest princeling
Had sent him packing.

He recalls clearly the scent
Of the lemon tree on the wind
Blowing across the imperial garden,
Bringing with it the harsh
Arresting voices of the Emperor's
Minions and the cold seizure
Of manacles.

As he muses on past events,
The ancient clock in the second
Room of his house in the gray
Sub-division of government
Buildings strikes three times
Too many: time-warp aberration
Han-shan has never learned
To correct.

Quick subtraction, however,
Sets the day right. At nine
Of the clock, the sun quarters
The fair mountain sky,
And Han-shan enters his garden.

His blue shirt is immaculate.
Twigs of white embroidery
Enliven the collar like sudden Snowfall.
He is still a fastidious man
And one of studied preference.

For example, the planetary perturbation
Of a peacock feather keeps his place
Where he has stopped reading
In the Analects. It bends the window-
Wind like the signal of triumph.
Shi-te once said, "The Indian bird."

Noon is Han-shan's quitting time.
Before he leaves the garden, he inspects
Again his sweet onion beds and his rows
Of prized early potatoes for any
Omissions he may have made.
All vinery is tied with yellow ribbons,
All king-posts are secure.
All is in order.

On the way back to the house, he picks
A basket of lacquered bramble berries.
"These," he says to his absent
But constant household companion,
"Will make an eloquent pastry
For our anniversary tomorrow."

Smiling through his tears,
He adds in all fairness, "Books
Are excellent for supposing, proposing,
Exposing, and deposing argument, but love
Is superlative, too, wherever
It may chance to be."

REVENANT

Han-shan tries to confine his
Lover's absence to the bedroom
But inevitably encounters

Shi-te in the long hall that goes
Down to the kitchen or sitting on
The backstair mending a bamboo fan,

Or re-weaving an old straw shoe.
At times, Shi-te gazes back at him
From the well when Han-shan peeps

In to see the reflected moon.
Once, when Han-shan had gone,
At midnight, to attend the new calf,

He heard his old friend laughing
Merrily out behind the barn.
Most Frequently, however, after a rough night,

Han spies Shi-te in the morning,
Scattering handfuls of broomseed
Among the flock of white hens.

YEARS LATER

Han-shan remembers wistfully the mystery
Of the white house on the hill,
Whose mistress had asked him in
When he came selling blackberries.

How beautiful he thought the hallway
With its shining floor and antlered
Hat rack. And how embarrassed he'd been
By his rough clothes and broken shoes.

He never told his mother, who would
Have scolded him for breaching the castle:
Not in the house they moved to next,
Nor the next house nor the next.

Always these houses had a broken window.
In one, the floors were planks laid
Unnailed on the clay. How he had rocked
His way from door to table to bed!

In young manhood, he heard the white house
Had been torched. The news hinted at murder.
Once again he was the boy selling berries
And glancing up the stairway where mystery resided.

III

REVIEW

"I'm laughed out of court
As I was once before"
Han-shan says to the crows
Observing his garden:

"What a fool I was to imagine
I could add my name to the
List of local masters.
I owe my friends an apology

For calling the young upstart
Critic in town a dunce
For naming my book the work
Of a country bumpkin.

I'm growing a bit thin-skinned
In my old age. After all the fellow
Is only trying to make his way
In a wood of thorns.

My prized sonnet there
I had imagined the equal
Of any in the kingdom,
But now it seems written

By a simpleton,
And my prized haiku
Dull as disaster
As I read it now:

Where went its incomparable
Wee pen-knife sting?
How distempered the lotus,
And creaking the bridge

Over the yellow river."

PREFERMENT

Once, Han-shan fondly remembers,
He was considered handsome enough
To carry yellow parasols for great
Officials at the far away capital,
And, what was better, allowed to post
One of his poems in the best part of town.

This was especially rewarding on holidays
When crowds followed in the wake
Of the magisterial procession,
Stopping to admire his haiku on the way,
And pointing him out with applause.

And he was indeed handsome:
Forehead as smooth as a garden leaf,
Eyes dark as charcoal,
Ears taut and pink as fanshells
Under hair the color of government ink.

Most proudly, he recalls the mouth,
Firm and curved as a petal
From the imperial plum.
And O, the nose rising like a young tower
On a palace meadow, and the wondrous sleek
Symmetry of a well-trimmed beard.

No wonder he had caught the Emperor's eye!

Here, on Exile Mountain, he lives on a road
No one uses, and when he tacks a poem
To his broken gate, it flutters
Unread in the wind.
His temples are veined now like spice melons,
Eyes wan as chestnuts long out of husk,
Ears like small wilted cabbages.

And O, the nose pitted as honeystones,
Mouth squashed as mashed mulberries,
Beard scragged as winter-blown clover.

SPRING FESTIVAL DAY

Han-shan drowses, sleeps,
Dreams, wakes, drowses,
Sleeps, and dreams again:

Along the Imperial Road
Into town, ribbons trail
From lamp-posts, and interweaving
Their colors, and the wayside
Grass is starred with silk
Flowers. Somewhere, lively
Music is playing.

Another Festival day has come:
Time for wistful poets with trembling
Knees, to stand before the people
And read the first fruits of genius
Among booths of cabbages, berries,
Melons and sweet onions.

Around them rise the other,
Less metrical cries of commerce.
Buyers and sellers make bets
On who will win the Poetry Prize.
A young man called Cold Mountain
Is among the favorites.

The rough rickshaw will soon
Be passing along the avenue
And holiday will begin at three
Strokes of the imperial bell.

Cold Mountain's mouth is dry,
His heart throbs in his throat.
Shi-te tightens his arm about
His young friend's shoulder.
A horn sounds. In the distance,
People begin to shout:
The New Emperor is arriving.

The tumult awakens Han-shan.
The morning sun is still low.
Aureate curtains ripple in
And out the open window.
A faded saffron robe lies across
A chair. From the lamp-stand,
Brown and turquoise, green, lemon,
And amber belts string
Like banners for holiday.

Han-shan tries to recall
The words of the first poem
He had read in public:
"Autumn came early that year…"
Is all he can remember
Before he drowses and sleeps
And dreams and wakes and drowses
And sleeps and dreams again.

The Festival

I

Back home from the capital,
Where his poems had been most
Gratifyingly applauded,
Han-shan recalls with pleasure
The man who had smiled at him
In the public rotunda.
How good it is, he thinks,
To travel.

II

At the festival
A man rushed out of the crowd,
Saying both Han-shan's name and his own,
Seized the poet's hand, exclaiming
That he, Han-shan,
Was a hell of a good poet
And vanished. Remembering,
The tired old man smiles
At being home again.

III

Thinking of the days spent
In the maze of the capital,
Guarded by his publisher's son
Wee Willie, Old Han-shan
Rolls himself into a ball
Under his own coverlet
And smiles and goes to sleep.

IV

Back from the festival
Where he's been for a day
A celebrated performer,
Han-shan grins wickedly to himself
Because he won't have to leave his mountain
Again for another year.

V

Waking the morning after
His return from the great festival,
Han-shan remembers the beautiful youth
Who had seemed to be singing
"Softly and Tenderly"
Just for him.

VI

Sitting among his retinue of poets,
Brown, Hardin, and little Wills,
Who is better than six feet
Out of his shoes, old Han-shan
Views his family with pride.
What better get could he have gotten
Than these, and without all that nastiness?
Two of his sons are brown-eyed, like him.
The other has eyes of the purple mountain
Whose peaks loom in the far distance
Behind the state house.

VII

In his own bed the morning after
The festival, Han-shan thinks: "God,
What a place of kindness the world is!"
He has not grown hungry yet.
His round belly purrs like a cat.
When he curls around it,
It becomes a security pillow.
He thinks how variously
Metaphor may attend the same event.
Beginning to feel alive,
He swings his legs over the side of his bed
And composes a poem: A limerick. As usual,
It is of the questionable kind.

OCTOBER

Han-shan wakes delighted.
Why, he cannot say.
He picks his mind for reasons.

Yesterday, at the town's festival,
He had paused at the door
Of a little shop he admired
And walked on without entering.

Could it be that he is no longer
In the market for yellow bowls?

STILL LIFE

Han-shan loves receptacles,
There being nothing lovelier
Than something with something
In it: a bowl of walnuts,
A bottle with old playing marbles,
And so on. He admires especially
The crow feather stuck in a worm-
Hole in his wall with which he teases
An ear in passing. How saliently
Delightful! Once, inspecting his
Treasures, he found a dead mouse
In the well of a chalice. "I must
Have not had anything to put in it,"
He said. "How wonderful of nature
To abhor a vacuum as much as I do."

ARACHNE

Hilling the garden squash,
Han-shan recalls the time
He spent with his old friend
On Other Mountain.

What a revel he had made
On the drums while Shi-te
Danced in his best robe.

There is a time to be sad
And a time to be glad:

Still, he reminds himself,
It behooves one not to be
Excessively merry.

He had returned to his house
To find a lace doily investing
The doorknob and the keyhole
Stuffed with oddments of silk.

And on the verandah, dead from
Exhaustion, the housekeeper
Lying where an errant wind
Had dropped her

At the end of a remnant of thread.

MUSIC

Han-shan sits on a flat stone
In his garden and plays the flute,
Mimicking the birds singing among
The gourd vines or from the top
Of the blue pine tree.

Or he constructs a new trellis
For the rambling rose over his front
Gate or works at the great loom in his porch,
Weaving his own coverlets.

Sometimes, he paints drinking gourds
To hang at his cold spring.

His poems, delicate but strong,
Paper the ceiling above his bed,
So he can lie and read
Always in reach of masterpieces.

No man, he avers, can catch
Such fish in one basket.

THE GARDEN

Just how many times, Han-shan wonders,
Has he used the clematis on the fence
To shield himself against public derision.

Soon, he tells himself, when he has time,
He must set bamboo at the clothesline
And another stand of the flourishing stuff
Between the house and the road
So he can visit longer with the postman
Without embarrassment.

Landscaping has become his specialty.

Now he gathers his robe about his waist
And squats in the peonies by the gate
To relieve an old man's propensities.

If a neighbor happens along,
He will nod and smile and pretend to be digging
Among the pretty flowers,
Hearing for the thousandth time,
"What a splendid garden you have!"

DROUTH

Squeezed in foreskins rolled tight as iron,
Okra pods grow phallic in the garden,
Hardening in the hard light.

As always Han-shan weeps for the infant ones,
Paralyzed in their bracts, stifled
Before emergence, into the first glory.

The birds come with immaculate feet to the bath
Skimmed with dirty water. When they fly again,
Their white feet become paradigms of mud.

The Postman, (O God, the Postman), stops
At the gate, ponders the number on Han's door,
Shuffles his letters and goes, leaving nothing.

All things are unfinished:
Heart's pulse, love's instrument foreshortened,
Withered pod. All day the raincrow has cried for rain.

OPTIONS

Han-shan lets his hair grow long
Until his friends scoff and advise
A barber. He also omits furnishing
Out his one half-eyebrow with a dark
Pencil to match it with the other
Unless his friends remark the absence.
There are few mirrors in his house.
When he stops before the small wall
Glass, it is to admire the gold
And blue cup on the shelf above it.
He does what he is bidden to please—
Whether to look normal or escape
Notice, he is not sure. The choices
Seem one and the same to him.

COMPENSATION

"Even at today's prices,"
Han-shan says, "my pension
Is still sufficient to provide
Good paper for my poems,
Especially if I use
The backsides of pages.

Thanks to having been
Courier for rich men,
Now, without benefit
Of rickshaw or horse-cart,
I am still able to get
To the river and bring home

A string of April fishes
And a pocketful of river-
Jumbled stones for the silken
Nests I've woven and hung
In the four corners of
This little house."

Upon Opening His Gifts on Christmas Eve

"Look!" Han-shan cries to the balanced cock
Peering in at the window. "Instead of reams
Of foolscap and quantums of onion-skin,
Here is a traveling case of embossed
Leather and a pocket compass
For finding my way about the garden!

Instead of stout needles and drums
Of mercerized thread, not to mention buttons
Of polished shell to hold my coat together,
I receive a brush for my bald head!

To what grand reception for my poems
Shall I wear this mock-gold chain
With the imperial image stamped
On the clasp as if I were still
Included in the royal favor?

And here, God be adored, is
An alarm clock. O, great snowbird
Teetering on the windowsill, what
Gross insult to your clarion call!

My new poems will again have
To be written over last year's pages
And, what is worse, with ruined pens!
Quadruplicate on triplicate on duplicate!

Already lines show through themselves
Like ancient palimpsests badly scumbled:
Fore- and back- shadowed adumbrations
Of financially-estranged genius!

This," Han-shan roundly declares,
"Is the saddest day of the year:
O, most disobliging, most melancholy,
Most sinistrously deplorable
Day of the year!

Such words recover the old poet's sense
Of humor: Han-shan is beginning to smile.
From where his house is on the edge
Of the crag, he can see far out and below,
The golden town most goldenly glowing.

"I can manage," he reassures himself.
"Weevils in the rice-sack are of little moment.
Things will improve when spring comes,
And Shi-te returns, bringing
In abundance all things we need."

TROUVÉE

The first letter of his name
Is a dollar sign without bars,
A reversed musical cleft,

A snake's delicate backbone
Twisted across autumn brown leaves.
Yet, for all the semiotics,

He is penniless to the point
Of penury (head rhyme being only
Another poor profit), cannot

Properly carry a tune (not knowing
One note from another, finding it
Impossible to raise his voice

At the octave's demand),
And left only with the charming
Gratuity of chancing upon

This Christmas morning
A snake's ivory spine in the last
Year's leaves of an old wood.

In All Fairness

It is true to say that Han-shan
Delights in memory to the extent
Of finding himself delighting not
So much in memory as in the theory
Of remembrance as rarefaction
Of mind to the extent of infinity
It's mindful to say the least
And an equal extinguishment of
Boundary. On certain days, the dear
Old man follows his nose into what
Was never on earth or in heaven:
Which is to say that memory
Is the profoundest of lies
And that Han-shan in his deepest reverie
Never told a whopper in his life.

OLD NEIGHBORS

Han-shan shuffles his sore foot
To his watching-post at the window.
He is on time and so is she.

Shears held carefully behind her back,
She humps along like a great spotted
Bug with pincers.

(Heaven knows, she's pocked enough!)

Snip. Snip. She seldom takes more
Than two of his precious peonies.
Today, three in retribution.

(There are various ways of being neighbors!)

Han berates himself roundly for not
Fixing the broken flag in the garden walk.
A turn of the shovel would have sufficed.

Each morning now she brings him gruel
And carries off a freight of flowers.
The year he had warm weather pneumonia,

It was the season of chrysanthemums,
And she had countered his complaint
By reminding him of the sagging gate

That disturbed her afternoon nap-time.
He should have repaired the damned gate
And canceled her voice at the outset.

(There are so many distinctions of cunning!)

Han-shan attempts to stamp his good foot
And winces. Feet are so companionable.
When he tries to relight his cold pipe,

There is no tobacco, no rushlight,
No pleasant fumes to enliven the house.
Soon he will have no peonies.

(God, to be dependent on a woman!)

A Hole in a Cloud

Heretofore in my life, Old Man,
I lived in twenty-three apartments
Of one sort or another,
Never content, moving from street
To street, house to house, room to room.
Somewhere, I was convinced, there
Was a place I could truly call my own.
But my conviction has faded.
I no longer dream and am no more
Than a tramp along the highway.
Here on Exile Mountain I've built
A nest in a hole in a cloud,
Being that kind of bird
And no longer a fledgling.

The New Biology

It almost causes me thrombosis
To think I'm only symbiosis:
A chimney stack of small communes,
Each dancing to its unique tunes,
Oblivious of the harmony
Which, Old Style, they said, was me.

NEWSCAST

Han-shan listens indignantly
To the latest news from the capital:
Legislators there have voted to do away
With the Man in the Moon, and the Speaker
Of the House is roundly declaring
That Humpty-Dumpty is no longer of use
To the people.

"Soon," Han murmurs sadly,
"Old King Cole will be deposed and Jack
Horner's Corner will be pronounced off-limits
To children under thirteen unless accompanied
By their parents. Old Mother Hubbard
Will be caught stock-piling bones and Betty Blue
Hauled off to court for wearing one shoe."

Any day now Han-shan expects a runner
To come announcing at his door
That the law protecting little boys
Under the haystacks has been repealed
And Old Mother Goose herself
Put in a government nursing home
Where she is kept under strict surveillance.
Furthermore, anyone found in possession
Of her politically incorrect Book
Will be brought to justice.

Foreseeing all this,
Han-shan keeps his copy under the sticks
In his woodbox, "No one," he thinks, "will think
Of looking there even though tinder
Attracts fire." The old poet is delighted
With his metaphor.

Each night, after he has condoled
With Lucy Locket over losing her pocket
And complimented Kitty Fisher on returning it
With its ribbon still around it,
Han hides his Book under the carelessly
Arranged woodpile and goes to bed, happily
Saying, "It takes a poet to fox the Grinch's men."

THE COUP

"Though summer is short, preference
Is shorter," Han-shan says. "I'm growing
Old. Soon there will be no time for me
To be recalled to the capital to read
In the Emperor's presence and have
My poems displayed on walls the entire
Length of the Royal Mile when he goes riding."

"There has been a change in power,"
Say travelers crossing Exile Mountain.
"The Crown Prince has seized control
Of the new government. Even now,
At this very hour, servants are busy
Preparing the cottage at the foot
Of the garden for the advent
Of the next poet laureate."

Han-shan's heart is gall as he remembers
The yellow ricebird in the lemon tree
And the perfume of a thousand flowers
Blowing in the open window.
And O the strawberries, the melons,
The cool cucumbers on the hottest day!

He stirs the soil around the solitary
Peony in bloom in the wooden tub
He calls his garden and brings
Water from the rainbarrel.

"Surely," he thinks, looking far down
The hill road to where the postman grows
Larger, climbing up to him:
"Surely a letter will come today."

"Han-shan! Han-shan!" the wind rises
Among the blue pines, chanting his name.

Rumor

When he heard that his name
Had been set forth in public
As being that of a great but
Neglected poet of the 20th Century,
Old Han-shan fell to
Laughing and wept until his
Yellow bowl of lentil soup
Adulterated with tears.

THE INVITATION

"It is not necessarily axiomatic
That he who kisses first
Kisses last," Han-shan writes
In his daybook....

The letter shakes in his hand:
He reads on. Now that the father
Is dead, the son declares me
Poet Laureate of the Realm
And bids me to return quickly
To the Imperial City
And resume my formal duties.
He has underlined his request
To hasten my obedience,
Adding, "While time and fondness
Hold," saying in so many words
That we are old and speed
Is imperative: always with him
A savor of philosophy.
I expect that since it was I
Who taught him.

Time is arrogant. The truth
Is in the mirror. How many years
Has it been since we were boys
And I dared intrude a kiss
On that high winsome cheek?

Han-shan scatters extra grain
To the audience of white hens
Hungrily flocking about his feet.

Is the lemon tree still leaning
Above the pool in the sunlit garden?
His voice as clear as birdsong
Among the scented branches?
He is old too,
I must remember. Questions beset
Han-shan about his various duties.

Will I be able to resume fitting
Fit words into fitter poems
In his praise as I did then and raise
My voice to the notations of near-
Forgotten songs and newly arrived-at
Meters as I did then to cheering
Crowds while ignoring country cousins
Yodelling derision outside forbidden
Gates. He smiles at the memory
Of the yawling boys, now so far away,
Ruefully thinking, "I can't carry
Even the simplest tune now."

Recalling that his physician declares
Him a marvel of fitness, Han-shan cries
To the startled hen: "The Emperor is dead!
Long live the Emperor!" Yes, I will return:
Walking together, we will personify
The arrival of a new age and announce
The presence of a universal good heart.
Arm in arm we will talk again
In a well-kept garden. And if any
Kinsman acknowledge me, I will honor
And esteem him above all others as partner
To accompany me in my journeys.
"I will go," Han-shan says.

But not before I have restored my own
Desemene to order: rooted out as weeds,
Tightened the loose stones in paths
And walks, recreated the old order
In visible design and pattern.

I would not wish the prince to visit
Me now: with thistles on every hand,
Brambles in tangles to tear his robe,
And locusts with their murderous thorns.
I must scrub these molding flagstones
Around the blackened fountain
Make of this country seat
The jewel it once was.
There is room in the Analects
For further precepts:
Even starving hens never find
The last seed.

The hens flow out and in again
Like seething water.
"There are times and seasons," Han-shan says,
Casting a final handful of grain.

"And there will be in the new heaven
And new earth," he says, "peacocks flying
Among the trees, making with their
Planetary wings a new constellatory of planets,
Dragging new universes from bough to bough,
Sweeping up old means and ways
Where comets seldom come to inquire."

UP FRONT

Han-shan owns but one suit,
A famous green he wears on
All occasions, his shirt a pale
Yellow, whether from age
Or delicate choice, who can know
Beyond the longevity of actual
Witness? His tie is a sliver
Of beryl on a field of orpiment
And falls straight as a stream
To the nub of his buckle at fall's
End, a bleb of silver overlaid
With good gold. When he stands
To read a poem to a barefoot audience,
He speaks of topaz melons in frames
Of virent vinery, of citron moons
Ensnared in tall pine trees, of apples
Of gold in green mountain mist.
He always finishes to a light tapping
Of applause. But Han-shan doesn't mind.
He is the year's Poet Laureate.
No one would dare raise a voice
In his august presence. Besides,
He enjoys rubbing the country's nose
In the real stuff.

RETURN FROM EXILE

On an April morning towards the end
Of the first decade of the fourth quarter
Of his life, as Han-shan kept time,
The Postman came with a letter
Bearing the Imperial Seal,
Bidding him back to the beloved cottage
At the foot of the Royal Garden.

Han-shan recognized the handwriting
Of the young prince, now grown into
The imperial position.
Remembering the yellow ricebird
In the lemon tree and the berries
Terraced among the peony flowers,
Han-shan bade the young man read.

In his loudest voice, the postman read.
"Come back, dear friend. Your
House is waiting for you."
Han-shan retired to his bamboo alley
To laugh and weep together,
Remembering the great strawberries among
The clamorous flowers.

"I'm going home," he said to the
Whispering grass. "I'll read again
In the Emperor's presence to great
Applause, and my poems will be posted
Along the route of Great Processions.
What a day that will be!"
How he would lean on the Emperor's arm.

Whereupon, the old poet tossed his worn
Robe onto the ragheap and spent all his
Savings on a new yellow one, bright as gold,
A yellow sedan chair, and sound
Sandals for the men who would
Carry his sedan chair over the mountain
Roads back to the capital.

MOTE

Every morning of late, Han-shan
Has cried into his rice bowl,
Knowing that he will never be
Clear-sighted again until he removes
The silverfish embedded in the eye
Of his grandfather, whose portrait
Hangs above the breakfast table.

COLD WATER

Born with a hankering for fine
Things but with the smallest of purses,
Han-shan had from the start to drink
Spring water instead of choice tea,
Wear roughest weave of pantaloons
In place of caterpillar silk,
And make his own shoes of short straw,
Always doing without exotics in his fare.
Even the local travelers crossing
Exile Mountain with a few goods to exchange
In town offer him little option
Except in the matter of love.

IV

COMMENTARY

My life has been little more
Than a long and difficult
Circuit in a small place
Famous for mountains.

Taught to make two bites
Of one cherry, in my old age
I am buffeted Ulysses
Reduced to a tightly told tale

Of axle and spindle.
Even my least words
Are dense with riddle,
Oblique with equivocation,

Shot through with paradox.
No Penelope would ever
Have understood me.
No Telemachus ever fathomed

The ways of his father.
No wife nor son have I
To sit in judgment on me.
There was, however, among

My companions, one Shi-te,
A mild man who worked
At the quarry and came home
Nightly, smelling of rock-dust

And singing snatches of song.
Dearest of all men,
Shi-te has been gone now
Above twenty years.

The Traveler

Each morning before he gets up
To feed the chickens and milk the cow,
Han-shan, propped among pillows, studies
The map of nameless places and lost
Addresses he keeps in his head:

He might as well consult the veins
On the back of his gnarled hand
Or count the rows of hair
As if they were tree-lined avenues,
So little information they give.

Somewhere in the maze of twists
And turns that leads his mind nowhere,
There is a valley of melons
And groves of plum trees:
Somewhere between mountains.

Farther, at the foot of an abrupt
Plateau, there are plats of yellow
Poppies that vie for attention:
But where? In what precinct?
What county?

And where, in what latitude,
Under the first snow of the season,
Stand the young chestnut trees
That make so viable a plantation?
Where the venue of chestnut-fall?

If there were only a fingerpost
Or marked stone on the river-road
To go by! If only he could remember
The man who gave him directions
With an ivory-ringed hand.

Mists open and close like swept
Curtains, denying further inspection:
At the barn the young calf pleads
To be turned in with its mother.
The old mare drums a door

With impatient hooves.
There is a sudden outcry
Among the white hens.
Firstlight is not the time
To reckon foreign geographies.

Or tabulate the years in an age.
Yet as his feet grope in bedside
Darkness for his scattered shoes,
Han-shan wonders if in that other
Realm the wheatfield is still on fire.

Han-shan Fashions a Myth

The old poet loves peacock feathers
And gathers them as they fall, one
By one, from perches in the trees
Near his house.

First, he caresses
Them with a dry writing brush, oh, so
Carefully, lest he separate the delicate
Spines, knowing the colors are interlocked.

Then, he looks for a place to stand them
In his cramped, little house. Proper
Location, he says, is half of any art.
Near his bed he keeps a jarful of
These planetary perturbations.

In the egg-yolk light of his lamp,
He sees universes scintillating in blue
And gold like his beloved Saturn,
And hears, from close by roosts, the dry
Clattering of galaxies being re-arranged.

And then the cry of damnation comes:
He sleeps and dreams of starfalls
And all the rumpus of dragons.

Hearing Aids

In sound silence
Han-shan holds them
In the palm of his hand:

As teeth from a dragon's
Jar of extravagations:

As lugs a mudwasp contrives
To hold a future in:

As wonderbeans bought
At the store of a magician:

As anything the imagination
Takes them for:

Not least, as studios
Of remembered sound,

Connectedly enlarging the timbre
Of a voice heard once

In another garden.
More than that, letting in

Through open windows
The lull of water quickening

Empty basins:
Or, from another room

In the same house, a violin
Playing Brahms,

And, at the same time,
Permitting the yellow bird

In the linden tree
At the bottom of the hill

To mix over and over
Again its golden bravura songs

In the whole orchestra
Of encapsulated delights.

PRIORITIES

Octogenarian though he may be,
Han-shan prides himself on his
Steadiness of mind: his hand may
Shake and spill his load, the world
Make its noise behind closed doors
In rooms lined with cotton wool,
The written page grows distant, and,
Worst of all, his robe stay damp
From the urgent bladder old men
Suffer, yet he manages to respect
Himself still. He keeps his head.
That's the important part. "Not
Until I fail to know the pisspot
From the waterjug," he avers,
"Will I have cause to worry."

NIGHT OUT: HAN-SHAN AT EIGHTY-TWO

In his garden at moonrise,
Han-shan ponders
The scandal of parroting
Going on in the capital,
Where, he's told,
The literati have become
Mere copiers, extractors of tidbits,
Especially the poets, who,
In consequence,
Are shamelessly embroiled
In counterfeiting and in crying
Infamy over who said what first.

Han is perplexed at the news
Yet he feels a certain sympathy.
"So many likelihoods
Are possible," he muses.
"After all, a man's genes
Take after each other.
I borrowed my own big ears
And sharp nose
From those who have gone before.
It's a rule of the world.
Even the garden bell rings
Changes on the same old ding-dong."

The moon hangs clear
Of the tallest pine
On Exile Mountain. "There,"
Han says, "is purest mimicry."
He nods, reflecting on reflection.
"Cast and copy!"
The owl uphill,
Listener of a thousand nights,
Hears him exclaim.
"Reiteration steadies the wobbling world!"

Thinking tires him now.
Before he falls asleep among Melon flowers,
To any watcher watching,
His head becomes only
Another white peony in moonlight.

FINAL EDITION

On his eighty-fourth birthday,
Han-shan receives a letter from his
Publisher, requesting a catalogue
Of all his works: *from alpha to omega,
From i to izzard*, the letter reads.

Angered by the tone and the indignity
Of being required to go through
A lifetime of papers heaped on the floor,
Letter in hand, dismayed, the old poet
Spins round and round like the dasher
In his ancestral churn, kicking as he goes.

Nothing accrues from the agitation
Of irreducible clutter: no dated card,
No postal cancellation, no faded obituary.

At last! here is a poem to autumn.
But which autumn among the many he had
Sought to appraise: anastrophe
Apostrophizing epistrophe without end?
But to what end? His poems are timeless already
By virtue of his own unconcern.

He must remember to say that to the publisher
In apology for the Syllabi and Indices
He had failed to keep.

In the name of his beloved Shi-te,
What mundanities are to be expected
Of a laureate, as though he were of no more
Significance than a book-keeper: secretary
Of bundle and bale: a common enumerator!

A rake from the underfloor, a shovel
From the garden, a manure fork from
The barn might help to simplify matters.

Han-shan groans at the prospect.
Scattering a sheaf of yellow pages,
Demeaning the corporate man in town,
He declares: "The miller shall have his toll.
That is but fair.

But where in the lovely concourse
Of earth did all this multifarious
Dreck come from?"

ANCIENTRY

These days, at broadest noon,
Han-shan has sleep in his eyes:
At the well, tiger lilies
Are blobs of indistinction.
By the gate, peonies are white
Ducks circled on the grass,
Inert as silence.

All the world draws faintness.
Once piercing eyes hardly
Prick the nearest distance:
Han thinks of an old gray horse
He once saw browsing upmountain
In September mist.

LULLABYE

Drawing up his knees
Until he curls round
His own umbilicus,

Divested of the world's
Wooing and wedding and
Wounding, imagining

Himself afloat
On the waveless pond
Of his mother's belly,

Han-shan tries to sleep,
And almost succeeds
In the stratagem:

But just as the last whisper
Of water dies in his head,
Wolves enter from the forest,

Howling nightmare.
The ruse has failed before.
It will fail again.

But not now.
Now he lies and stares
At green-fire eyes,

Conveners of night journeys,
That have followed him in
From the wilderness of day:

Now his mother sings
The sleep song and his father
Hunts faraway in an empty wood.

EARLY SCHOOLING II

Han-shan remembers going to school
At the capital with so many other
Shans, the master called the roll
By first announcing the category
And then bawling out numbers as if
He taught accounting. On the roster
Han's name was Number Seven: a digit
He still hates because its head
Is always bowed, and he despises
Humility almost as much as he
Despises arithmetic. How dreadful
To have his poem attributed to Seven,
As if he were no more than a cipher!
How could such a number ever further
His career? Even now, here on Exile
Mountain, he can't escape public
Opprobrium. In his dreams
The master still bawls his number,
And Han wakes shuddering, seeming
No more than another nought in
His already threadbare coat.

DELUSIONS

I

In the evening, old Han-shan speaks
Cheerfully of the past: how as a boy
He made wooden birds fly, snared frogs
In summer water-meadows, and climbed
Trees with two inseparable friends.
And of how later, at the capital,
He won fame for designing great houses
And writing excellent poems.
He is lying, of course.
The truth is, his path was lonely
And mud-pelted. And when he went to town,
Thinking to better himself, instead of mud,
He had queer words flung at him.
Retired now on Exile Mountain,
He recalls a time he could not
Possibly remember.

II

Sometimes at a memory party
When Han-shan is asked to speak,
He is greeted by chuckles from the other
Guests and wonders, since he has yet
Said nothing, what the laughter is all about.
The old man has been to too many soirees,
And listened too well. The history he
Recounts is not his own. Even the others
Cannot remember whose story it is.
So they laugh, too, at their own expense.
Han-shan, however, is most confused
Over what is his and what is not.
The moral is that old men who wish
To keep their accounts straight should
Keep out of too much evening company.

TWILIGHT

Twice already since darkness,
Han-shan has answered his door
When no one was knocking:

Rattle of wind, rustle of doves
In the yard-tree, sound of autumn
Nuts falling on the roof-top?

The world talking in its sleep?
Only late fireflies flash lovelights
In upmountain distance

And accusative katydids begin
Their endless accusations:
Did she? Did she not?

Walking out to the great stone
Outcrop that leans above the valley,
The old poet empties the dregs

From his wine-cup into the air,
Wondering how a vacant heart
Can break from too much fullness

NIGHTFALL ON EXILE MOUNTAIN

Bound for the rookery in the tall
Pines, crows enter the evening air.
At the cliff's edge, looking down,
Han-shan ponders nightfall,
Speculating dragons in the caves
Of the valley below, where, he likes
To think, the scaly tribes are
Gathered, snorting fairytales.
Black mist curls at his feet.
Soon, his head floats momentarily,
A white peony in a black bowl,
Before it, too, is eclipsed.
Farther up the mountain, among the peaks
Behind him, autumn trees flare
Like festive rockets, going out,
Snuffed to the last leaf.
How reiterate, Han muses, admiring
The ways of ritual. Repetition
Has become his only guarantee, his
Sole assurance. "All that rises
Must fall," he says for the thousandth
Time, like a scriptural verse,
In incantation of order and arrangement,
Confident that darkness will withdraw
Into its dragon lairs in the valley
After the crows have slept.

CATCH-ALL

Han-shan often dreams of falling
Off cliffs and rooftops and into rivers,
Always quite conscious of never reaching
Bottom. Waking, he reasons that under
The earth—far, far away, on the other side—
Is the world again. "One thing supports
Another seriatim," he thinks. "If I fall
Out of the world, the earth will catch me."
He caresses his bed. "So far, I've managed
To keep a good straw mattress between
Me and elsewhere." Stepping into his
Reasonable shoes, he lines a basket with
Old scripts and goes to hunt the eggs.
On his way to the henyard, he stops
To stone the sparrows digging in the herb
Garden, smiling at the way the earth
Palms the pebbles. "If I gave them
Free access," he wonders, "how long would
It take the pesky, little souls
To reach the antipodes?"

DREAMS

Now, when Han-shan's father comes
Into his son's house, he asks:
"What place is this?
Have I been here before?"

He leafs through a book,
Gazes at a picture on the wall,
Parts a curtain at the window.

Han-shan looks up from the poem
He is writing and answers
As he always does:
"This is your home, sire.
You've lived here since
You went away."

Then he offers his guest
A cup of moonlight
From the crystal bowl he keeps
On the windowsill.

MELVILLE

For Han-shan's father

Smoke from his father's pipe
Stung Han-shan's nostrils like dry
Cedar boughs burning in the winter
Woodlot long before the pleasing
Stench knocked his father to his knees
In attitude of prayer, the axe
Still gripped in his hand.
He was carried home in his own
Straight-backed chair.

A crow was attracted to
The caterwauling men, but no sea
Eagle came clawing at the top
Of the tallest tree left in
The grove while he drowned in
His own maelstromic blood.

Han-shan says,
"All stories end differently alike.
That is the only truth I've ever
Been able to salvage from the wrecks
Of literature I've traveled on."

THIS MORNING

Getting out of bed, Han-shan
Falls flat on his back between the bed
And the bureau for the second time in a week.

He lies breathless, feeling no dismay, only
A sense of expectation confirmed: "I'm
Developing an intimacy with the earth,

The old leveler," he says, getting his breath
Back. "The world keeps going for my head,
The love of one sphere for another," he
Supposes. "With heaven kicked out of the way."

He smiles at the egregious metaphor
And climbs the bedpost to a new erection,
But tempted to slide down again. Stepping
Gingerly, he makes his way to the kitchen,

Wondering how many more falls he will be
Obliged to take before he is forced
To accept the stance and keep to the level.

THE WILL-MAKER

Han-shan likes manuscripts
And writes with many a flourish,
Serif, and uncial, drawn flowers
Between the lines and unicorns
Rampant in the margins.
The sheer beauty of a text enthralls
An old man who studied calligraphy
In the best writing schools
Of his day.

So he rewrites his testament incessantly:
"Here beginneth what beginneth here,"
He begins his weekly recapitulation
Of the precious instrument:
Always smiling as though the false
Palindrome had just occurred to him.

"I direct," he continues, "all objects
Of worth found in my boxes and jars
To be dispensed among my several
Lovers in the order of their arrival
At my house on the day of my funeral,
Of which they will have been duly apprised.
The last shall receive the best.

There is one, however, who will not
Come until the second day, having
Had to walk far through forbidding country.
Save for him the finest ring
In the ring box.
Forgive him his muddy clothes.

There is, too, in the butter-dish
On a shelf in the spring-house
A legacy of old gold. Give him that
Also because he is poor."

There will be, Han understands,
Changes of mind: erasures of codicils,
Names added and subtracted in what
He calls the art of giving and taking
Away: arithmetics of love.

He may even decide to liquidate
All his assets and spend the proceeds
On a sumptuous meal for his ne'er-do-well
Attorneys who are too honest
To make a living.

Thinking of what he may yet bequeath
And to whom, Han dips his stylus
Into the yellow pot, and writes:
"Here beginneth what
Beginneth here."

SUNDAY

Sundays are not especially welcome
At Han-shan's home, not this Sunday
Especially. He lies late in bed,
Grumbling, scolding his empty house
For not containing voices. Then he
Remembers he has been asked to go
And see his friend, the dead man,
At the funeral home in the next valley,
And brightens up a bit. After all,
He thinks, there are days and days,
And puts an extra spot of rouge
On each cheek.

REFLECTION

At the funeral of his old friend,
What could have been more natural
Than Han-shan's sudden chuckle
At the ancient brown face coated
With rice powder and resembling
Nothing more than a crayoned land-
Scape under snow: relief map that
Was itself relieving?
Yet no one understood.
Thinking him gone daft,
Other friends led him to the spring
For a cup of water. Kneeling as
Before a mirror, and seeing another
Face staring back at him through
Realms of glass, Han-shan laughed
Louder than ever.
Still no one understood.

ANNOUNCEMENT

Han-shan is writing a letter
From his ship in the harbor.
"We have just passed
The estuary light," he says.
"The sails are furled.
I am Ulysses coming home
From the last great voyage
Among the pig-sties and lotus
Eaters. Come to meet me, Shi-te.

Around me the sailors slump
With tiredness from their encounters
With contrary winds.
No screech of windlass haunts the air.
No straining ropes sing with taut
Necessity. The endless round
Of continuity is over.
The harbor waters are still.

We are older men now,
Edging the age of elegies:
Bereft of former strength,
We are men, nonetheless,
Though fit now only for gardens:
Cabbages, mints, melons and sweet onions,
And the ineffable goodness
Of summer berries.
The movable feast is not yet over.

We shall dine together still,
My dear patient brother,
Despite the rough tenacities
Of increasing weather.

I see ashore the little house
Almost hidden in the cove of pine trees:
I am coming home again
To my wife, my son, my aged father.
Do not smile at this, Shi-te.
We have been all these to each other.
Is blind Argus still living?

I am much changed but much
The same still, being part only
Of all that I have met:
More chagrined, perhaps,
Less ashamed at failure,
More reluctant to spill
A brother's blood,
Having a greater capacity to love.
A man is always more than
What he becomes.

Standing at the bow
Of this pretty ship, looking
Beachward, seeing sand grains
Roll in and out, I think,
If I listened closely
To what the wind is saying,
I could hear the sirens
Singing their beckoning song.

Meet me at the turn-stile,
Shit-te, old comrade,
And lead me hand to hand
Up the white seastone path
Once again, safely across
A familiar threshold.

HAN-SHAN ANTICIPATES HEAVEN

On that first day when we must walk
In gaits we are not accustomed to,
Making the mis-steps of strangers,
Going not as angels go,
Half-dancing, half-flying,
But stumbling in the clearest street,
Falling where no obstacle is,
Bruising our heels in unbroken shoes,
Tripping over untied laces
To the titters of wonted angels
Who have assembled to see us fail
In our run for the roses,
How shall it be that we are not
Permitted to utter a few faint damns
At our celestial awkwardness
In memory of the gentle earth?

MINISTROKE

Han-shan's face burns like the look
Of electricity on a stove's eye:
Then the heat turns to gray ash
On a dead burner.

He tries his hand to see,
But his hand is blind.

How quiet the world grows, he thinks,
Watching an ant's progress
Across the arctic expanse of the cabinet door
Above his head.

He names the insect *Ross* after a man in a book
He once read about death in a white place.

By and by, the ant reaches a crack in the door
And tumbles down the crevasse.
Only then does Han-shan crawl to his feet
And try to act as if nothing has happened.

A Writer's Credo

Han-shan says:
"A poem must be so
perfected in itself
that it offers no problem
to the common reader.

Otherwise, the writer
should maintain a journal
in line with a local
intelligence not
exceeding his own."

HOLLYHOCKS

Now that he has grown old
Han-shan has time alone
To consider loneliness:

I've nothing about me
In this papery existence
To recommend company, he thinks,

Except the tall hollyhocks
Outside my curtained window
White and red and so deeply

Purple they appear black
In the silver air that comes
Here in the early morning.

Those who pass by to see
The stately flowers cannot discern
The man behind the curtain,

Where inside paper walls
And poems beginning to fall in strips,
He is learning the difference

Between loneliness and being alone:
How the one comforts and the other
Eats at the heart strings

And brings a melancholy of spirit
He cannot fathom, beyond the sounds
Of a tall tree shaken by wind:

Leafless in spring
And leafless again in autumn
When passing birds come through, going

South in company, twittering in
Excitement at the prospect
Of arrival again where hot sun is,

And there are blossoms
And warm rains and hopes of futurity,
And a companion to sing back

The pleasures of being.
These paper walls will shake again,
Bellying in and out, reminding me

Of poems I can no longer write,
And meters I have forgotten:
And hollyhocks, now blooming

So forth-rightly, will thin again
To papyrus, and I will sit, alone
To warm the small fire on the lonely hearth.

REVENANT II

Now, in the evening; you come,
Han-shan, to dictate a poem
In a growing calendar of days.
You are slightly tipsy and stand
Before me with your hands behind
Your back, rocking to and fro
On your slippered feet.
You have, you say, just had a good
Laugh at the moon and are still
Smiling faintly at the liquored joke.
Your voice is low and when I bend
To catch your words, I see
A purple dragonfly fanning
Its wings on your bald head.

THE GIFT

"Doubtless," old George says,
Resting on a roadside stone,
Examining his bruised heel,
"Doubtless, I encountered
Tertium quids in depicting
Han-shan's life as mine,
Seamless as the account
May seem now to others.

Given to ups and downs,
Crooks and bends, turns
And tumbles,
Foreshortened by rain,
Running away up to the sky
In fair weather,
Roads are much the same
All over.

All journeys end at the beginning.
All travelers arrive home
At the moment of leaving.
Han-shan was a taker of roads
Speaking doubtless in his unrest
Clever and excellent words,
Pronouncing the Way.

Like all of us,
He often slept on stubble,
Stole apples from forbidden
Orchards, purloined melons
From proscribed gardens,
And, when standing before Herod,
Wet his hose and other garments
As, doubtless, being old,
Herod was wetting his.

What wayfarer walks
Without seeing the local hills
Turn purple as bird-wings,
Or sudden star-flowers,
After storm?

All men tread the same ground,
Experiencing sunrise and sunset,
The same astonishment of first love,
Grievous as the screech of grief
Over a splinter thrust
Under a fingernail.

The glory of memory
And the rapture of recognition
Are universal.

Seclusions notwithstanding,
All third things forgiven
I've invested a fabled poet
With an immediate presence,
Furnished a good man a good life."

Carefully, Old George adjusts
The cloth about his injured heel,
Marveling over the chromatics
Of extravasated blood.

EPILOGUE

FAREWELL

I have a gift for you, Han-shan.
It's nothing you can use.
It won't bring you a dime
Nor can you give it to another
Like a ring or a fine coin.
You would be ashamed perhaps
If I told you what it is.
Here is a riddle:
Why does one old man cry
When another, his friend,
Shakes hands and goes away?

—*The Author*

About the Book

This book was typeset in Bembo which was modeled on typefaces cut by Francesco Griffo for Aldus Manutius' printing of *De Aetna* in 1495 in Venice, a book by classicist Pietro Bembo about his visit to Mount Etna. Griffo's design is considered one of the first of the old style typefaces, which include Garamond, that were used as staple text types in Europe for 200 years. Stanley Morison supervised the design of Bembo for the Monotype Corporation in 1929. Bembo is a fine text face because of its well-proportioned letterforms, functional serifs, and lack of peculiarities; the italic is modeled on the handwriting of the Renaissance scribe Giovanni Tagliente.

The painting of Han-shan and Shi-te in the front of the book is by the Chinese artist Yan Hui, also known as Yuang (1280-1368).

The cover photograph by Lori Kincaid of a wind-swept tree was taken on Max Patch Mountain in Pisgah National Forest in North Carolina and frames Round Mountain in Cherokee National Forest at first light. For more information visit: http://www.kincaidphoto.com.

—Jo Stafford

George Scarbrough was born in 1915 in a clapboard cabin in Patty, a small community in Polk County, Tennessee. He was the third of seven children in a family of sharecroppers which moved frequently around the County during his early years. Strongly influenced by his literate mother, he was an avid reader from his earliest years, and showed literary inclinations which seemed very strange in the County at the time. He attended The University of Tennessee in 1935-36, The University of the South in Sewanee, Tennessee for two years on scholarship during the war in 1941-43, and then taught in several Tennessee schools. He entered Lincoln Memorial University and graduated with a B.A. degree cum laude in 1947. He received a masters degree from the University of Tennessee in 1954 and later attended the Iowa Writers' Workshop. He moved to Oak Ridge, Tennessee in 1968 to be with his ailing mother and lived with her until her death in 1983. He published poetry in more than 65 magazines and journals over many years. He also published five major books of poetry and one novel. He received a nomination for the Pulitzer Prize for his last collection, *Invitation to Kim*. He died in December 2008. The George Scarbrough Archive, a permanent repository of his papers, is located at The University of the South.

CPSIA information can be obtained at www.ICGtesting.com
Printed in the USA
LVOW121417231011

251692LV00006B/1/P